MW01089526

Astrology

The Comprehensive Guide to Using Zodiac Signs and Horoscopes for Better Relationships, Becoming Wealthy, and Life-Long Success

SECOND EDITION

By
Janet Ritchie

Table of Contents

Introduction

I want to thank you and congratulate you for purchasing the book, *Astrology: The Comprehensive Guide to Using Zodiac Signs and Horoscopes for Better Relationships, Becoming Wealthy, and Life-Long Success.*

This book contains proven steps and strategies on how to use zodiac signs and horoscopes to improve various aspects of your life – relationships, finances, and success.

The book also gives a brief look into the history of astrology, discussing the earliest references to astrology. You'll also get to meet some of the famous names in astrology. However, aside from astrology, the book also provides valuable information on horoscopes, and how you can seek guidance from it as you go through life.

Thanks again for purchasing this book, I hope you enjoy it!

CHAPTER 1

Basic Things to Know about Astrology

Astrology is a branch of science usually defined as studying the positions and aspects of heavenly bodies. It further studies the influence of these movements on physical occurrences on earth and its inhabitants. The word "astrology", when mentioned, is oftentimes met with smirks or indifferent reactions because most people do not know that much about astrology. What is astrology and what are the basic things that one must know about it?

It is interesting to note that despite little knowledge about astrology, people can easily name their astrological sign. It just shows that behind the lackluster acceptance of its merits, people find some truth in the way the cosmos moves. It is used to explain why unusual things happen and why certain feelings come out. All these can be understood better if people had interest in astrology.

A Quick Guide to Astrology

The word "astrology" is usually grouped with the concept of superstition, the paranormal, mysticism, and the occult. Many still think of it this way without considering the fact that astrology has been with man since early history. It was even thought of as similar to astronomy because both use the same reference table in doing their works. One who is an expert in astrology has extensive knowledge of the stars and other bodies that occupy the enormous space in the universe.

Astrology teaches that there is a center within every human creation. That center refers to man's essence and is symbolized by the sun, the center of the solar system. It further claims that the movement of the sun since our birth dictates our essence. That is why astrologers use the horoscope, from the combined words of hour and scope, to gain an insight into our lives as they are influenced by celestial activities.

As a system of belief, astrology claims that there is a connection between natural phenomena and human events. By means of the horoscope system, astrologers can read a person's personality and predict his future using the position of the heavenly bodies as reference.

The development of the science of astrology can be attributed to the Greeks. They are responsible for coming up with 12 groups of constellations, which, in astrology, is termed as zodiac from the Greek word for "animal." Each zodiac is named after a particular characteristic that personifies each of the constellations. Astrology offers man an instrument to know his personality and tendencies as he weaves himself through many probabilities. It exposes opportunities and challenges and gives advice on how to counter dangers.

Astrology in Daily Life

From astrology's viewpoint, humans are not puppets pulled by a string. It teaches that we have free will that stops at a certain point, and then we can decide which path to choose. The responsibility lies entirely on us. That is where astrology comes into the picture. It asserts that it can provide man with an insight of how things are going to be. Astrology helps us understand how to use the best of our potentials and be the best of ourselves. Because we are prepared with the probabilities, astrology allows us to shine and excel in situations that are otherwise difficult to meet.

Astrology can be an accurate tool to ascertain if energy forces are favorable or against us, especially if we are trying to make some decisions. It generally serves as a guide for us to interact with people around us. It can help us create a happier life because knowing about astrology is having a better knowledge of ourselves. Together with the sun, moon, and the stars, astrology is mainly about us.

Now, let's take a trip down memory lane as we explore the origin of astrology.

CHAPTER 2

Digging into Astrology's Past

The origin of astrology is obscured with antiquity. Regarded as a sacred science, it was studied with what is considered its twin science – astronomy. The rich records of astrological history were the oldest astrological documents gathered from different ancient civilizations with different astrological systems.

Science was born during primitive times when man was relating life's occurrences to a more powerful force than he. Needing an answer, man started linking everything with what he perceived as responsible for his destiny: the heavenly bodies.

Man started to record and give interpretations of his experiences. He started to base his insights on the celestial bodies having invisible influences upon life on earth, particularly that of the human being.

The Start of Astrological Documentation

The period between 668–626 B.C. produced the earliest astrological documents, which record observations of the solar and lunar movements. These documents contained astrological calculations and predictions. As early as 410 B.C.E., Babylon recorded horoscope charts or birth charts of its citizens. Used by the early man to guide him in his daily life, these documents are now useful in digging into the history of astrology.

The ancient records reveal that eastern civilizations refer to the stars as bearer of news. Even the Bible contains some fascinating stories about bright stars guiding the prophets in fulfilling their mission. The Biblical story about the Magi who went to visit the infant Jesus caused some to believe that they were actually Persian astrologers who used the North Star to locate the birthplace of the prophesied Savior.

The Emergence of Astrology from East to West

The introduction of Western astrology to ancient Greece started from ancient Mesopotamia around 600 B.C. The period was characterized by the flourishing Greek civilization and the rising popularity of the first Greek philosophers. By the time Alexander the Great has conquered and Hellenized the world between 336–323 B.C., Egypt became the established civilization of Hellenistic Greek philosophy. It was during these times when the scholars began to study and develop the science of astrology.

This period witnessed the birth of the horoscope and the zodiacs. Much later, Hellenistic scholars played twin roles. They served as mathematical astronomers who scanned the celestial for intergalactic movements and metaphysical astrologers who interpreted and linked these movements to human events. Many relics that continue to rise from their ancient grave only confirm that astrology and astronomy were part of the Eastern and Western culture.

The Application of Astrology

In using what is available to retrace astrology history, it can be proven that even during the early times, astrology is considered a science with useful application. During that conservative time, astrology was the domain of the priesthood. It is used in their place of worship to speak to their gods and ask for healing. Rulers and conquerors used it to advance their interest and in formulating strategies for defense and to stay in power.

Up to the last centuries, astrologers served their western rulers in determining propitious dates to hold important events during their reign. The long road down astrology history lane passed through a chronology of events that lead us to where the science is now placed in the lives of the people. At present, it is no longer exclusive to the whims of the sovereign and the powerful. It is within the reach of even the lowliest of citizens.

It is applied for both complicated and trivial purposes that include weddings, opening a business, weather prediction, and more. Nevertheless, the most popular is probably obtaining self-analysis. With astrology, one can have a better understanding of his own personality. This makes us all a little nostalgic once more and as we review the path of how astrology affected our lives, it makes us realize that we are all part of its history.

The next chapter will introduce you to some of the famous names in the field of astrology.

CHAPTER 3

Getting to Know Some of World's Famous Astrologers

Many articles had been written about the science of astrology. When asked, a person can probably say something about the subject but knows little or no information at all about the personalities who made predictions that changed the course of history. These people are called astrologers. According to Wikipedia, an astrologer is one who is engaged in the practice of one or more forms of astrology. His typical job is to draw a horoscope of a certain event and to make an interpretation based on interplanetary points and positions.

Some of these people became famous astrologers and became part of human history because of their impact to the society. To be recognized in the field of astrology takes more than drawing a birth chart and making an accurate interpretation. Famous astrologers obtained their name and fame because of their extraordinary accomplishments, contributions and associations with other famous historical figures. Some of them are the following:

John Dee (1527 – 1609) - John Dee is referred to as the Queen's Conjurer because of his association with Queen Elizabeth I of England. He lived during the Renaissance period and was considered an accomplished person in other fields other than astrology. He was also a mathematician, astronomer, and geographer. Being an astrologer, he also delved on the occult and studied it alongside science. He contributed greatly to the Scientific Revolution.

Johannes Kepler (1571 – 1630) - Johannes Kepler is of German descent who specialized in astrology, astronomy, and mathematics.

During his time, the science of astrology was studied with astronomy. He was credited for his works that led to many scientific discoveries including his famous theory on planetary motion laws.

William Lilly (1602 – 1681) - This famous English astrologer specialized in interpreting astrological charts. He excelled in horary astrology, which is the study of the skies to generate answers to certain questions. He was involved in a controversy regarding one of his predictions. He foretold of the Great Fire of London in 1652. It took 14 years before it actually occurred. Some people accused Lilly of starting the fire to make the event happen according to his prediction.

Evangeline Smith Adams (1868 – 1932) - Evangeline Adams, a famous American astrologer, is known for the many books she wrote about astrology. She established one of the earliest consulting businesses engaged in the science. Because of her fortune telling activities, she was arrested twice. The story goes that she gained an acquittal after giving the judge an astrology reading.

Marc Edmund Jones (1888 0 1980) - Another American astrologer, Marc Edmund Jones is a notable figure in American astrology. He was also a screenwriter whose aim is to regain the image of astrology as a serious and rational science. During his time, astrology was mostly treated as a fortune telling activity. He is responsible for writing many books on astrology. He is claimed to have co-authored astrology's Sabian Symbols.

Jeane Dixon (1904-1997) - The most famous astrologer in American history during the 20th century, Jeanne L. Dixon is credited for her unforgettable prediction about the assassination of John F. Kennedy. She also authored many books including her best-selling biography. She became more famous because people can read her minor predictions through her syndicated astrology column in one of the leading American newspapers.

These famous people are being honored and given a place in history because of their significant contributions and accomplishments during their time. Presently, many scientists have the makings of becoming famous astrologers. A big difference can be seen between them and the well-known astrologers in the past. If today's astrologers can make accurate readings about themselves, they will be able to see the time when the spotlight is on them, being revered as great astrologers of their period.

The next chapter will discuss astrology as basis of horoscopes and will get you acquainted with the different horoscope signs.

CHAPTER 4

Discovering the Basis of Horoscopes

Zodiac signs and horoscopes managed to survive centuries of change. To this day, although most do not take horoscopes seriously, a substantial number of people still consult horoscopes and zodiac signs for their concerns. The basis of horoscopes and zodiac signs is the position of the stars and the visible constellations at one's time of birth.

Astrology

Astrology is the basis of horoscopes and the zodiac signs. This ancient field is devoted to the movements and relative positions of celestial bodies (such as the Sun, Moon, and planets) and their influence on human life. Based on the movements, and the relative proximity of these heavenly bodies, astrologers perform divination. Through this, people will have a guide when deciding about business, marriage, children, and projects that they may favorably undertake.

The Western zodiac signs are actually considered spatial divisions of the heavens. They are also attributed with influence and given prominence according to their placement in the sky and by their angles relative to one another. The modern application of astrology is found in the zodiac signs that are supposed to hold sway over people born within the time when the specific constellation is visible.

Horoscopes and the Movement of the Stars

Astronomers and astrologers believe that the destiny and life of a person can be seen through the movements of stars, planets, and other heavenly bodies present in the galaxy. In the same manner, the astrological aspects and sensitive angles of the stars can chart a person's fate at the time of his birth and other significant life events.

The Egyptians and Mesopotamians had already developed zodiac signs and horoscopes by 2000 B.C. These were used to mark the seasons through the constellations we now know as Taurus, Leo, Scorpio, Aquarius, Aries, and so on. These constellations also represented the twelve equal segments or divisions of the zodiac.

Many people believe that celestial phenomena influence and even determine human activity. This is founded on the adage that what happens in the heavenly realms is reflected on what happens below. This is partly the basis of horoscopes and the twelve zodiac signs used to represent the twelve basic human personalities.

The Zodiac Signs

Based on the belief that the movements of the stars influence human life, there is a strong relationship between the time of year a person is born and that person's personality type. People born under a particular sign are assumed to have basic characteristics that they share with people born under the same time of the year. The twelve signs of the zodiac form a kind of "clock" that relates directly to the sun's position as the earth journeys through the heavens in an orbit or cycle that takes one year to complete.

This is why the different signs of the zodiac are sometimes referred to as sun signs. The following are the twelve constellations with their Latin names. These names are still used by many people and astronomers today:

1. Aries, the Ram (March 21 – April 19)

2. Taurus, the Bull (April 20 – May 20)

3. Gemini, the Twins (May 21 - June 20)

4. Cancer, the Crab (June 21 – July 22)

5. Leo, the Lion (July 23 – August 22)

6. Virgo, the Virgin (August 23 – September 22)

7. Libra, the Scales (September 23 – October 22)

8. Scorpio, the Scorpion (October 23 – November 21)

9. Sagittarius, the Centaur (November 22 – December 21)

10. Capricorn, the Goat (December 22 – January 19)

11. Aquarius, the Water Bearer (January 20 – February 18)

12. Pisces, the Fish (February 19 – March 20).

These are the common zodiac signs and horoscopes that are still used today. Many recognize these symbols and accept personalities that they attribute to those born under them.

Valid Horoscopes for Contemporary Life

Ancient societies and astrologers believed that life on earth is greatly influenced by the movement of the celestial bodies. Moreover, they believed that much of a person's character and destiny was determined by the alignment of the planets, moons and stars at the time of his birth. Today, many people still believe that the stars influence human life and that they can provide guidance through horoscopes. However, for every person who believes that destiny is written in the stars, three times as many people challenge the idea that there is a thing as valid horoscopes for contemporary life.

The Question of Validity

The issue of horoscope validity is one that has been around for a long time and will always be difficult to answer. Although the readership of daily horoscopes remains consistently healthy, many people will say that horoscopes are nothing but superstition because regardless of the amazing calculations it takes to track the astrological movement of planets and stars, there is little scientific evidence to show that the predictions derived are anything but supposition.

How a Horoscope is Created

There is a system to the task of creating a horoscope. Seers and fortunetellers may rely on their personal gift of paranormal sight but this does not hold true for horoscopes. The astrologer must first ascertain the exact time and place of a person's birth before creating a horoscope for him if the reading is designed to make a personal forecast. There are times when the prediction is needed to assess the success or viability of an event. In this case, the astrologer must know the exact time the activity will be initiated.

Once the time has been ascertained and expressed in Universal time, the astrologer has to convert this into the appropriate sidereal time and consult a set of tables called ephemeris to find out the location of the sun, moon, and planets at the specified time concerned. From there, other information has to be obtained and based on these, calculations have to be made.

The product of all these will be a clear illustration of which stars and planets are rising, visible, and are hidden at the time of birth or at the time an activity is initiated. The astrologer then makes his interpretation based mainly on accepted characteristics or powers attributed to the stars. Partly because of this painstakingly complex process and because of the existence of set and consistent formulas, many people will say that there are valid horoscopes for contemporary life.

The Bottom Line

What horoscopes predict may or may not come true. The bottom line is this: there is a 50% chance that what horoscopes say will happen, but there is an even stronger likelihood that what a person believes will come true. It is probably safe to say that horoscopes become valid not because they are always right but because belief in them makes people behave in ways that render the prophecies self-fulfilling.

CHAPTER 5

Getting to Know the Horoscope Signs

In the previous chapter, we discovered the basis of horoscopes and we briefly discussed the 12 signs of the zodiac. Now, we will get to know more about each of them.

The most popular horoscope signs are the signs of the zodiac. These are based on the position of the stars during the different times of the year and are actually names of the constellations visible at specific times. The signs of the Zodiac can give great insights regarding day-to-day living and the many talents and special qualities people possess. You can discover a great deal of relevant information about yourself by reading about your Zodiac sign.

Aries, the Ram (March 21 – April 19)

Of all the horoscope signs, the sign of the ram is the one with people who are creative, flexible, and insightful. Aries people can be ambitious and driven, often making them over-achievers in whatever they set out to do. They can also be impatient, but because they are devoted friends, lovers, and family members, they are always well loved.

Taurus, the Bull (April 20 – May 20)

Taurus people have strength, stamina, and will. They are stubborn by nature and will stand their ground to the bitter end. Sometimes, they will do this beyond reason. People born under the sign of Taurus have a softer side. They are loving, sympathetic, and appreciative.

Gemini, the Twins (May 21 - June 20)

People born under the sign of the twins have flexibility, intuitiveness, adaptability, and balance. However, they tend to have a duality to their nature, which means it is sometimes hard to predict how they will react.

Cancer, the Crab (June 21 – July 22)

Cancer people are home loving and family centered. They are devoted to family and are most at home in domestic settings. They are comfortable with tradition and because the moon rules them, they can be moody.

Leo, the Lion (July 23 – August 22)

The zodiac sign of the lion is all about leadership, power, and exuberance. People born under this sign are natural leaders. They can also be high-minded and vocal about their opinions. Many of the horoscope signs represent people with strong personalities but Leo is the one with the strongest leadership suit.

Virgo, the Virgin (August 23 – September 22)

Virgo people have sharp, keen minds and are they are wonderful conversationalists. Often, they can easily convince others of outlandish tales. They are inquisitive and are good at drawing information from people.

Libra, the Scales (September 23 – October 22)

Libra people care about balance, justice, equanimity, and stability. They like to surround themselves with beauty and harmony but can sometimes go to extremes to do so. With Venus as their ruling planet, Libras are very understanding, caring, and often the champion of underdogs.

Scorpio the Scorpion (October 23 – November 21)

The Scorpio is often misunderstood because they are bold and are capable of doing ambitious things with a cool, controlled confidence. They can overcome considerable obstacles when they put their mind to it.

Sagittarius, the Centaur (November 22 – December 21)

People under the sign of Sagittarius are thinkers. They have an outstanding ability to focus and can be very intense. However, they have the tendency to go in too many directions at once. Learning to channel their energy is a big challenge for them.

Capricorn, the Goat (December 22 – January 19)

People born under Capricorn are highly intelligent. They know how to apply their knowledge to practical concerns. They achieve their goals by purposeful, systematic means.

Aquarius, the Water Bearer (January 20 – February 18)

The Aquarian is gentle and assuming, going about accomplishing goals in a quiet, often unorthodox way. Aquarians are the humanitarians of the zodiac. They are honest, loyal, and highly intelligent.

Pisces, the Fish (February 19 – March 20)

People born under the sign of the fish are unassuming. They like to keep a low profile and often have quiet dispositions. They are honest, unselfish, and trustworthy. However, they can be overcautious and sometimes gullible.

The next few chapters will discuss how astrology (and horoscopes, too) can help people find success in love, business, and life in general. Let's first find out how you can find your soulmate through astrology.

CHAPTER 6

Finding the Perfect Soul Mate through Astrology Compatibility

It is often surprising to see two people who get along well when they seem to be the exact opposite of the others. On the other hand, it also makes us realize that these people cannot stand each other if they do not possess identical qualities and temperaments. It appears that the combinations of opposite and identical personalities serve as the best groundwork in having an almost perfect relationship. In reality, this is achievable through astrology compatibility.

In principle, astrology compatibility does not only work for people in amorous relationships. It also applies between friends, siblings, colleagues, and co-workers because there is also the need to know if we are investing our relationship with the right people. The first step in determining compatibility is to compare the zodiac signs of two people. Although zodiac signs are not enough, the logical system of grouping the characteristics in each sign are used to establish, gauge, and calculate the level of compatibility between people. In these groupings, intervals between groups end up being more compatible with the others.

The Different Types of Astrology Compatibility

• **Zodiac Compatibility**. This type uses the astrological analysis of the person. It provides a better understanding of the characteristics of people belonging to any of the twelve zodiac signs. It serves as a window to discover oneself. This method can prepare a person for marriage or can teach him how to relate with others. Using the different sun signs, the person can better equip himself on how to handle relationships.

• **Tropical Astrology Compatibility**. This effective method of evaluating the strength of the liaison between two individuals is achieved by revealing the intensity of the relationship they share. This is done using the sun signs. Compatibility is assured if both of their sun signs indicate the same characteristics and temperament.

• **Tropical Astrology Moon Sign Compatibility**. In astrology, the moon is one important factor in influencing compatibility. It is considered more important than the sun because the sun sign highlights the external personality of a person while the moon sign reflects his internal habits and instincts. Compatibility is said to be derived more internally, using the heart and innate tendencies of an individual. Moon sign is established based on the lunar position in any of the tropical astrological domains.

• **Astrology Co-worker Compatibility**. This is a method of generating working compatibility using the sun signs of Western Astrology. This can reveal how well you deal with co-workers in the workplace. Because we all have different working habits, this compatibility test can help you better understand working preferences by referring to your zodiac sign. The sun signs are said to assume a role in influencing your personalities and work choices.

• **Astrology Travel Compatibility**. You can be better prepared on how to coexist and deal with your travelling companions with this test. This can provide you with an insight regarding what you particularly like or dislike about traveling so that in your next travel, you can choose a travel companion who can easily adjust to your travel preferences. Again, this points to the sun signs as playing a role in shaping your decisions when making travel plans.

There is no such thing as perfectly compatible. There is always some degree of incompatibility that exists among people because mortals were created unique and special. However, when we try to have a better understanding of each other's personalities and temperaments, even the imperfect incompatibility can possibly work. Those who work have the illuminating light of the sun, moon, and stars to guide them in their relationships.

For those who find it difficult to make their relationship work, astrology compatibility comes to the rescue. The thing is, your soulmate isn't necessarily the person you get to spend forever with. A woman's soulmate can be a woman, too, a best friend. Therefore, the next chapter will show us if love and astrology really do mix.

CHAPTER 7

What's Love Got to Do with Astrology Love Signs?

In astrology, a love sign is the zodiac sign to indicate that Venus was present during the time of a person's birth. In Roman mythology, Venus is the goddess of love and beauty. In Greek mythology, she is named Aphrodite, the same goddess who symbolizes the qualities of love, sensuality, romance, and beauty. Being the goddess of love, Venus is used to gauge an individual's compatibility with the other astrology love signs. Her presence in your birth chart dictates how you deal with your relationships with others.

Astrology love signs, or love sign compatibility, indicates how your zodiac sun sign suits another person's zodiac sign. Experts claim that people's compatibility or incompatibility with others can be gathered from the date of their birth and zodiac signs. This is generally done by comparing the element group with the other group of elements in the zodiac chart.

The Effect of Zodiac Elements on Astrology Love Signs

Each zodiac sign is defined by the four elements of the zodiac. They strongly influence a person's romantic compatibility because they are deeply seated in our individual characteristics. People with the same elements feel relaxed with each other. Friendship is easily formed between two people who share the same elements, though this does not automatically turn into something amorous.

The zodiac signs are formed into the following groups:

- **Fire:** *Aries, Leo, and Sagittarius*. People under these zodiac signs are characteristically strong-minded, eager, demonstrative, and impulsive.

- **Earth:** *Taurus, Virgo, and Capricorn*. People born under these birth signs have the tendency to be materialistic, but they are also practical and focused.

- **Air:** *Gemini, Libra, and Aquarius*. Individuals born under these signs are classified as the intellectual and versatile type.

- **Water:** *Cancer, Scorpio, and Pisces*. Those belonging to this group are emotional and empathic but idealistic.

The fire and earth elements are self-centered, while the air and water elements have the tendency to be more considerate of others. Fire and air demonstrate optimism and free-will. Earth and water elements possess security, negativism, and passiveness. Each individual assumes these general traits but has the freedom to put a twist to make him different from the rest.

The Love Match

People feel comfortable with those with whom they share the same elements. If you are looking for a love match, find someone who belongs to the same element that is compatible with the element your zodiac belongs into. As an example, if your zodiac is Aquarius, your element is air. You are most likely to be compatible with someone who belongs to the fire element because both of you possess the same quality of optimism and free-will.

In finding a match, you may let Venus do the job because that is her realm: love. Venus' touch is felt in how you invest emotions in a relationship, how you remain in it, and how you break the ties. The presence of Venus determines your decision in choosing a partner. If your Venus is compatible with your choice, the relationship is bound to have a happy ending. However, differences in love signs can result to disagreements and falling-outs that make it impossible to become even just friends.

Even though you are unique in your own individual ways, people who belong to the other signs also influence you. You may find that not all the characteristics for your Venus love sign are apt to your personality. You are nevertheless sure to find a character trait that exactly portrays you. You can use these astrology love signs to guide you in seeking someone with whom you can feel comfortable. It is a good way to understand why people may do extraordinary things in the name of love.

CHAPTER 8

Horoscopes for Love and Compatibility

In Chapters 6 and 7, we discussed how astrology figures when it comes to compatibility and finding one's true love. This chapter will briefly discuss how horoscopes fare when it comes to both.

For centuries, people tried to use astrology and the zodiac to determine which person and actions are compatible and which are not. To this day, horoscope consultants are asked to find out if the stars will shine auspiciously on certain matches and certain decisions. Horoscopes for love and compatibility are a whole area of divination for zodiac experts.

Compatibility According to Signs

The task of using horoscopes for love and compatibility is a complex one because it is often not enough to use only the twelve zodiac signs as reference. For example, in theory, Aries and Leo are supposed to be compatible but in reality, they may be in conflict. On the other hand, Libra and Cancer may be theoretically incompatible but in reality, they happily stay together forever. Missing the possibilities of compatibility often happens when an astrologer or a horoscope consultant uses only the Sun Signs.

There are other factors involved in figuring out compatibility. For greater accuracy, it is far better to consider these other factors when predicting love and compatibility. When the relationship in question is a love relationship, the Venus signs should be studied carefully. This is because the Venus sign focuses on the individual's character in terms of love relationships and can therefore be exceptionally enlightening.

There is a special field of interest called Zodiac signs compatibility. This is useful in discovering more about a person's compatibility with family, friends, and colleagues. It is useful not only for matching two people romantically but also for putting together working groups or production teams.

Compatibility According to Personality

Astrology can be divided into natal astrology and mundane astrology. A natal horoscope is a chart, map, or imaginary snapshot of the planets in the Solar System and their positions in the zodiac at the exact time of a person's birth. Mundane astrology is the application of astrology on world events.

Astrology predictions may also be used to further understand the individuality of a person, his successes and failures, as well as to determine what his feelings and behavior will be over a particular period.

Individual horoscopes are compared to know how two people with different habits and characters influence each other. Will they manage to get along? Who will be the leader? What parts of their personalities will help develop the relationship and which will resist it? The stars and their presence at the birth of a person will give important information to answer these questions.

Affinity

The affinity between two individuals is known as compatibility, which is also known as Synastry, and is the study of the relationship between two individuals using a relative study of their natal charts. The relationship between their planet positions, signs, and houses is analyzed to determine the level of compatibility. The study is based on the distribution of energy on their individual and combined charts.

Compatibility between Zodiac signs can be based on Chinese astrology, Western astrology, or Vedic astrology principles. The planet Venus represents female force and Mars, the male force. When a male's Mars is in the same position as that of a female's Venus, then they show greater compatibility or attraction.

Those relationships really work usually have their Moon, Mars, or rising sign (Ascendant) in their partner's Sun sign, giving them common ideals and goals enough for the long run ahead.

Astrology comes to your rescue when you encounter some sort of relationship hitch.

No two sun signs are compatible. A degree of incompatibility always exists because that is how we have been made. The story of incompatibility started right from the Garden of Eden. No doubt, it exists between us mortals. Nevertheless, regardless of what horoscopes for love and compatibility say, understanding and commitment can make even the most incompatible relationship work.

The next few chapters will discuss how astrology and horoscope may be used to guide one in business and life.

CHAPTER 9

How to Go About Getting Business Horoscopes

In ancient times, major decisions in commerce were always made with the advice of seers, oracles, and horoscopes. Possibly because of the world economic situation in the past decade, this practice gained even more popularity. It is a tendency that comes from wanting to make sure that business will be conducted successfully. The number of businessmen who are interested in getting business horoscopes grows daily.

Philosophical Basis of Horoscopes in Business

The application of astrology and horoscopes to business is based on the belief that planets are the sources of clear and well-balanced instruction based on the laws of nature laws that determine what people are, and how they live and move. Fire, air, earth, water, animals, and humans are all subject to, and can be aided by, the movement of the planets - movements that cannot be separated from anything with life in it.

Studying the influence of planets is the key to knowing what a person and his dealings on earth will be worth and what he can do to prepare for life's occurrences. It follows, therefore, that the best way to reap maximum profit out of a man's material business is to make it conform to the astrological laws.

Applying Horoscopes to Business

Both Chinese and Hindu horoscopes devote much attention to business. Hindu business astrology, for example, makes recommendations regarding the most suitable business for an individual. It also indicates the good and bad times for implementing effective business decisions.

Business horoscopes address questions such as when it is auspicious to set up a business, what business a person should set up, when a businessman shall see profit, when the business should go global, and how capital can be built, enjoyed, and preserved. These horoscopes deal with the concern of disciplining every function of business to ensure that it becomes a successful enterprise by providing guidance on how the business can be run in cooperation with the laws of nature.

The business horoscope is derived from calculating business prospects from a person's horoscope. The combinations arising from an individual's horoscope are the basis for deciding which businesses are appropriate to pursue. Predictions are made after studying the important houses governing success in business in relation to the person's chart.

The Zodiac Signs and Compatible Fields in Business

For most astrologers, people will do well in businesses that are compatible with their zodiac signs and horoscopes are often specific in their recommendations. For example, people born from March 21 to April 20 would fall under the sign of Aries, the Ram. It is predicted that they will be successful in operations that involve securities and currency, cash operations and banking, road construction, and transport. At the same time, they will be vulnerable if they entered real estate, the procurement and sale of seafood, and the manufacture and sale of chemicals or varnish.

Another example is the prescription for people born from April 21 and May 20 (Taurus). The horoscopes based on planetary movements will say that they will probably find success in the sale of goods for apartment repair, sale of furniture, sale of real estate, construction, hair-dressing, fashion, and design agency.

They are also predicted to do well in automobile service, flower and animal cultivation, tourism, hotel service, and gaming business. However, Aries people are taking risks if they go into the manufacture and sale of medical and video equipment and chemicals.

Getting Business Guidance

The easiest way to get business horoscopes today is through online resources that often make free consultations available. Another way will be to buy software and use it to analyze the business decisions that have to be made. It is good to remember though that even if the stars may influence human activity, human effort, creativity, discipline, and many other factors also have much weight in determining the success of whether or not an endeavor will prosper.

CHAPTER 10

Giving Astrology Meanings to
Your Daily Life

Learning the science of astrology demands dedication when it comes to learning all its facets. It is exciting in the sense that astrology can reveal something more about you and other people you deal with. Half the fun of it is in knowing the different astrology meanings and later on, having that delightful feeling upon discovering that you aptly belong to a sign that perfectly fits your characteristics.

The beauty in understanding astrology is like being in a journey of discovering yourself and the people in your life. Having such knowledge can help you associate the meanings to yourself, family, friends, colleagues, and even strangers. It helps you adjust yourself with others, knowing that is how their signs depict them. To have a full grasp of these meanings, let us look at some of the most common astrology terms often encountered in learning about the science and art of astrology. Keep in mind that this is not the complete list because astrology encompasses a wider scope beyond words and meanings.

Zodiac and Zodiac Signs

The first thing that a would-be astrologer needs to do is to observe the sun motion as it moves against the stars. For an entire year, it becomes evident that the sun traces a large circle, which, in astrology, is called ecliptic. The ecliptic circle is also where the earth orbits around the sun. The thin band that can be found on either side of the circle is called the zodiac, which literally means circle of life. This explains why most zodiac signs are named after people or animals.

There are 12 signs in the zodiac. Each of them is 30 degrees long, not to be identified as time but blocks of space. The cycle starts on the ecliptic spot where the sun is located on first spring day. It begins with the zodiac, Aries. When a person refers to himself as an Arian, it means he was born when the sun is located in the zodiac of Aries. Our calendar is designed in such a way to simulate the sun motion around the zodiac. That is why the 12 signs are comparable to the calendar months based on the zodiac. In the calendar, the months represent time and not space.

Astrological Qualities

The zodiac signs are also formed into groups of four according to their distinct qualities of taking part in human affairs. These qualities are called Cardinal, Fixed, and Mutable. An element is assigned to each group. This means that in each element grouping, there is a sign with cardinal, fixed, and mutable qualities. Each quality is associated with the season. The cardinal signs herald the beginning of the season, the fixed signs stay while the season continues, and the mutable signs signal the end of the season and pave the way for the coming of another season.

- The first group is comprised of Aries, Capricorn, Libra, and Cancer, belonging to the cardinal signs. People in this group are considered self-starters of the zodiac because they have the qualities of being initiative. They have the potential of becoming excellent leaders and rulers.

- The fixed signs are composed of Leo, Taurus, Aquarius, and Scorpio. Individuals who belong to this group are the slow type but sure winners. They spend much time in deliberating before finally making a decision. They are steadfast and firm. It is just appropriate that they belong to a group that implies their characteristic as "fixed".

☐ The next group is the mutable signs with Sagittarius, Virgo, Gemini, and Pisces. People with this sign are open-minded and adaptable, and they welcome new ideas. They are quite adept in communicating. They possess interest in philosophy and cultural differences.

Being familiar with astrology meanings can make you better understand yourself and help give you patience with others. Instead of asking yourself why people act in certain ways, you are now ready with an answer. You can give it a shrug of your shoulder, knowing everyone is just going through a phase in life. Another season is ahead.

CHAPTER 11

Components of a Horoscope

You may have seen horoscopes that involve sun signs (ex. Sagittarius, Taurus, etc.) and predictions for each. Although these may be enough for some, they are not as accurate as those made for a specific person. This other method makes use of the birth chart.

The Birth Chart

The birth chart is a map of the sky at the exact time of a person's birth. It corresponds to the projection of the planets on the ecliptic or the Sun's yearly path. The birth chart depicts the qualities and potentials of a person, and it can be used to divine what may happen during certain time periods.

The subject of the birth chart is placed at the center of the birth chart diagram. The signs and planets surround him/her in a circle. This arrangement represents how the astrological influences affect the person at the moment of birth and all throughout life.

You can construct a birth chart by consulting tables of planetary positions or using astrology software. Either way, you can find something you can use online.

The Quadrants and Houses

During the time a person is born, the Sun is positioned in one of the zodiac signs and one of four quadrants that divide the day into equal parts. This arrangement determines the Sun sign and ascendant sign. These two decide the ways through which the solar sign are expressed.

The quadrants are as follows: the ascendant, imum coeli/nadir (depths of the sky), descendant, and mid coeli/midheaven (center of the sky). The ascendant is the sign on the horizon in the East at the time of birth. It explains how a person finds his place on earth, and describes how he relates to the environment and how others perceive him. The descendant is the sign on the horizon in the West. This symbolizes the person's relationships with others.

The horizon line separates space into two half circles, with the mid coeli on top and the imum coeli at the base. The MC represents the person's power and the IC his origins.

Each quadrant is divided into three Houses that correspond to a specific area of activity. Put together, these make 12 houses that stand for the various aspects of the subject's life

- First House: Personality, attitudes, appearance, health

- Second House: Assets, possessions, money, salary, energy

- Third House: Communication, thought, words, meetings, contacts, mobility

- Fourth House: Roots, family, ancestors, heredity, home, emotional, social, and cultural influences

- Fifth House: Creativity, expression, enjoyment, pleasure, romance, children

- Sixth House: Management, work, domestic life, discipline, illness

- Seventh House: Relationships, sharing, marriage, partners, adversaries

- Eight House: Transformation, change, crisis, sexual energy, subconscious, death, rebirth

- Ninth House: Intellect, spirituality, travel, discovering broader horizons

- Tenth House: Achievement, power, career, destiny

- Eleventh House: Friendship, group activities, social involvement, ideals

- Twelfth House: Internal life, introspection, secrets, mysticism, suffering

As you may have noticed, there are 12 Zodiac signs and 12 Houses. They are not the same, though. The signs are based on constellations while the houses are determined by dividing the ecliptic into sections that always start at the east. Another crucial difference is that the Signs affect the *way* the planets influence the individual, while the Houses determine the *area of life* where they will happen.

Planets

The planets embody your different components. Their locations and their positions relative to one another have effects on the subject.

- Sun: The sun symbolizes the ego, willpower, and consciousness. It may also depict masculine aspects.

- Moon: The moon represents the unconscious mind and emotions. It deals with your feminine or maternal aspects.

- Mercury: As the fastest moving planet, Mercury stands for movement. Thoughts, exchanges, communication, and skills are linked to this planet.

- Venus: Bright Venus embodies beauty, aesthetics, love, and harmony.

- Mars: The red planet is associated with your strength, fighting spirit, conquests, and virility.

- Jupiter: The largest planet of all, Jupiter symbolizes expansion, fulfillment, success, and generosity.

- Saturn: The ringed planet is about structure, concentration, discipline, and solitude.

- Uranus: For a long time, astrology included only planets up to Saturn. Thus, when Uranus was discovered, it was considered as a planet for breakthroughs, originality, individuality, and creativity. It is also assigned to modernity, technology, and electricity.

- Neptune: Like its name, Neptune is for deep things – artistry, inspiration, sympathy, dreams, psychic abilities, and mysticism

- Pluto: This planet symbolizes transformations, destruction, and rebirth, as well as nuclear energy and internal alchemy.

Aspects

The aspects are the positions of the planets relative to one another. Planets in aspect are determined by geometric angles and illustrated by lines within the zodiacal crown.

The measure of the aspect's angle is derived from the angle of the arc of the circle between to planets. The kind of angle will dictate whether the relationship of two factors are harmonious or not.

The planets may link to certain signs and Houses, thus forming many combinations of planetary actions in various life aspects. This may also reveal whether you have harmonious relationships or conflicts with those around you.

The major aspects are as follows:

- Conjunction: This is when two planets are so near each other that the angle they form between them is close to 0 degrees. This combines their energies without hindering their ability to cooperate.

- Sextile: The sextile is a 60-degree angle between two planets. This enables harmonious energy flows between them.

- Trine: The trine occurs when there is a 120-degree angle between planets. Again, this is a harmonious arrangement, which amplifies the positive traits of each.

- Square: A square forms when two planets are 90 degrees apart. This reveals conflicts or tensions between them.

- Opposition: The opposition occurs when planets are directly opposing one another. This highlights alternations or swings among their energies.

The minor or secondary aspects do not have as much impact as the major ones. These are the following:

- The semi-sextile is a 30-degree between planets. This is a milder form of the sextile and it is also beneficial to the subject.

- The semi-square is a half-square (45 degrees between planets). The sesqui-square is a little more than a square (130 degree). Both of these have energizing effects on the planets involved.

- The quincunx is a 150-degree aspect between two planets. This represents an obstacle to be overcome by the subject.

- The quintile is a 72-degree aspect and portrays creative impulses.

Transits

The transits are among the most important parts of Astrological predictions because they describe times of key developments and their related influences. These correspond to the planets' movement through sensitive points in the birth chart:

- Ascendant

- Center of the Sky

- Personal planets (Sun, Moon, Mercury, Venus, and Mars)

The transiting planet activates the potential of the point that it contacts.

The more personal the transited point is, the slower the transiting planet moves and the stronger the effect of the transit becomes.

For example, Uranus takes a lifetime to activate all birth chart points successively. This transit has important effects especially when it passes over the Moon. This leads to family changes such as marriage or divorce. Saturn can pass through every point in the birth chart three times. This brings life lessons on the aspect that it transits. Several planets in transit can simultaneously interact and link some points of the chart through specific aspects.

Reading a horoscope requires you to consider each and every element involved. This takes a lot of practice but eventually, you can quickly combine several factors to produce accurate interpretations. The next chapters will tackle each element more deeply.

CHAPTER 12

Planetary Aspects

The ways the planets affect each other have particular consequences to the individual.

Sun

The Sun is the most essential part of the person. This may also signify his physical body.

Sun and Moon

- The Sun is the conscious and the Moon is the subconscious.

- Conjunction: This means being born during a New Moon. The conscious will and subconscious mind cooperate well. There is the ability to focus strongly on what one chooses. This may also result to stubbornness.

- Sextile/Trine: The individual attracts luck and opportunities. He has an abundance of energy.

- Square: This means that the conscious and subconscious is in conflict, leading to dissatisfaction and self-sabotaging behaviors. However, this can be extremely motivating.

- Opposition: Sun opposite the Moon is a full moon. The person may be hypersensitive and restless. He may enter difficult relationships.

Sun and Mercury

- Because Mercury is about thoughts and communications, aspects between the Sun and Mercury reveal how well one can express himself.

- Conjunction: This aspect can give a quick mind. However, for those who have close conjunctions, this may also mean thinking too much of one's self.

- Semi-sextile: Mercury and the Sun are always close to one another so they can't form a trine or sextile. It can form a semi-sextile though, and this can slightly improve communication skills.

- Opposition: Likewise, Mercury and the Sun can't be in opposition to one another.

Sun and Venus

The interaction of Sun and Venus determines sociability, desires and the ability to attract them, and artistic capabilities. It can also pertain to resources and relationships.

- Conjunction: Attractive and affectionate, the individual craves for and thrives in relationships. He loves all things beautiful and pleasurable. This also brings talent for the arts.

- Semi-sextile: Like Sun and Mercury, Sun and Venus are also close to one another so they can't form sextiles or trines. This mildly enhances artistic talents

- Semi-square: This can create problems with sexual matters.

Sun and Mars

Mars is all about action – how intentions are acted out and how energy is directed towards goals.

- Conjunction: Having an abundance of energy and braveness, the subject is a risk-taker and adventurer. He is not afraid of competition and will fight when needed.

- Sextile/Trine: Energy is controlled. He is assertive but not aggressive.

- Square/Opposition: The subject finds it hard to manage his personal energy. He tends to put too much effort. He may also be impulsive and temperamental.

Sun and Jupiter

The Sun is a person's potential while Jupiter represents opportunities.

- Conjunction: The person is good natured, funny, optimistic and resilient, making him careless at times. This is because he tends to be lucky.

- Sextile/Trine: This is a fortunate aspect that brings success, health, and positivity. However, he may become unmotivated because things come easily to him.

- Square/Opposition: The negative side of Jupiter is its tendency to blow things out of proportion. This can make him egotistic and spend too much or overdo things.

Sun and Saturn

The Sun is the individual and Saturn is discipline. This combination reveals how he is tested and how he deals with it.

- Conjunction: A disciplined, responsible, and patient person. This makes him capable of overcoming obstacles, especially those brought about by a difficult childhood.

- Sextile/Trine: Carefulness, responsibility, and hard work create fortunate situations.

- Square: The subject may have low self-esteem because of internal issues.

- Opposition: Enemies and external circumstances challenge the individual.

Sun and Uranus

The sun is the identity while Uranus is eccentricity.

- Conjunction: A unique and unpredictable person, often highly intelligent and independent.

- Sextile/Trine: Freedom-loving yet flexible. Good luck may come into his life unexpectedly.

- Square/Opposition: The subject must guard against impulsiveness and rebelliousness.

Sun and Neptune

The Sun is the person's energy while Neptune is his wishes. This can lead to creative endeavors or impractical actions.

- Conjunction: An artistic individual who may have psychic gifts. However, he may have a world of his own, or be prone to substance abuse.

- Sextile/Trine: Intuition and imagination are used productively.

- Square/Opposition: He may have a hard time distinguishing fact from fantasy. The individual may be deceived easily or may deceive others.

Sun and Pluto

This shows how the person handles power and control.

- Conjunction: A strong and intense person. He may be dominating or be obsessed with something/someone.

- Sextile/Trine: Power is well-managed. There is deep insight and flexibility that leads to positive transformations.

- Square/Opposition: The subject is cunning to the point of being manipulative. He must avoid being drunk with power.

Moon

The Moon is the deeper part of the mind – the subconscious mind, emotions, instincts, and habitual behavior.

Moon and Mercury

Major aspects of moon and mercury points out to an intense need to express emotions.

- Conjunction: Intelligent and in tune with feelings, the individual is good with words.

- Sextile/Trine: Because of the harmonious influences, the subject thinks clearly and communicates well.

- Square/Opposition: The individual may be overly sensitive to criticism. He may also become hyperemotional and have an unusual mind.

Moon and Venus

Major aspects of Moon and Venus means there is an emotional need for beauty and love.

- Conjunction: A pleasant person who may be dependent on relationships.

- Sextile/Trine: Affectionate and with a preference for pleasant things, although sometimes can indulge too much on them.

- Square/Opposition: Romantic relationships may be conflicted; some may become clingy while others detached.

Moon and Mars

Since the moon represent emotions and mars is passion, those with major aspects between these two can express what they feel directly.

- Conjunction: Emotions are intense and may be expressed straightforwardly.

- Sextile/Trine: Energetic, helpful, and honest.

- Square/Opposition: Impulsive and bossy. Prone to mood swings and anger issues.

Moon and Jupiter

The moon and Jupiter combined can lead to emotional outbursts.

- Conjunction: A person who feels a lot and wants to help others, thus promising more than he can give. He will be the happiest with increased opportunities.

- Sextile/Trine: A kind person who helps others honestly.

- Square/Opposition: Problems managing emotions.

Moon and Saturn

The moon and Saturn pairing is about control on emotions.

- Conjunction: There may be a difficult past, perhaps with the mother. However, he can overcome this with self-discipline and practicality.

- Sextile/Trine: The emotions are managed well, thus, increasing chances of attaining success.

- Square/Opposition: He may be emotionally deprived. There may be issues with women, but he may overcome all these when time goes by.

Moon and Uranus

The moon and Uranus pairings create surprises.

- Conjunction: This can lead to unpredictable emotional reactions. This can also make him react in strange ways and have unusual experiences.

- Sextile/Trine: The person rebels against tradition and limitations. He is attracted to novelty and stimulation.

- Square/Opposition: The person may be easily distracted or attract problems. He may be aloof to others to hold on to his personal freedom.

Moon and Neptune

Neptune is about imagination and mystery while the moon symbolizes the inner parts of the person. This arrangement can strengthen fantasies or bring confusion.

- Conjunction: Ultra-sensitive of emotions of one's self and others, thus, he may feel too overwhelmed. This creates both kindness and vulnerability. The person may also have a strong imagination that he can express in the arts. However, he should avoid falling into substance abuse to escape from stress.

- Sextile/Trine: Because of kindness and empathy, the subject may be unable to say no to others. He may also be extra imaginative, which is good for creativity but bad for focusing.

- Square/Opposition: This creates emotional struggles and wishful thinking that may cause him to resort to substances. However, he also has creativity and sensitivity that he can use to overcome this hindrance.

Moon and Pluto

Intense Pluto interacts with emotional Moon and causes profound feelings and penetrating insights.

- Conjunction: Controlling, possessive, and sometimes stubborn. However, he can handle major transformations well.

- Sextile/Trine: The subject is able to cope with changes well. Emotions are purged periodically.

- Square/Opposition: Emotions are inhibited. The individual finds it hard to trust others, and he/she may take advantage of others' trust. Power struggles are frequent. Domestic problems may occur as well.

Mercury

Mercury stands in the person's ways of thinking and expressing thoughts.

Mercury and Venus

Venus' beautiful energy of love and beauty goes to Mercury's mental prowess when they are in aspect to each other.

- Conjunction: The subject is good with words and may talk a lot. Humorous and charming, he is a delightful communicator.

- Sextile/Trine: An excellent communicator who is also a diplomat.

- Semi-square: Mercury and Venus are near each other so they can't form a square or opposition. They can form a semi-square though, which can encourage him to be more creative yet critical of loved ones.

Mercury and Mars

Aggressive mars and intelligent mercury combine to form a formidable mind.

- Conjunction: The subject is a good debater, with strong beliefs and the ability to defend them well.

- Sextile/Trine: Thoughts are spoken quickly and honestly. He can make sound decisions on the spot.

- Square/Opposite: There is a tendency to commit verbal abuse and lash out.

Mercury and Jupiter

Expansive Jupiter influencing intellectual Mercury can lead to big ideas or excessive distractions.

- Conjunction: He can see the big picture and be open-minded about most things. He is also an influencer of others. Since Jupiter also deals with happiness, he may be the happiest when he gathers new information.

- Sextile/Trine: The subject is interested in a lot of things and is a master of persuasion, although in a good-natured way.

- Square/Opposite: There is a tendency to be careless in making conclusions, and in exaggerating details.

Mercury and Saturn

Saturn is the planet of control and structure. When interacting with Mercury, this can create an individual who is disciplined with thoughts and can apply ideas into action.

- Conjunction: There is an air of seriousness around the person. He thinks logically and prefers practical knowledge over frivolous ones.

- Sextile/Trine: Has an organized mind with good focus.

- Square/Opposite: May take things too seriously. He may also be inflexible and prone to depression.

Mercury and Uranus

Uranus is an attractor of original ideas. Mercury and Uranus aspects are commonly found in geniuses and madmen.

- Conjunction: This generates insights and ideas out of the blue. The person also has unique ways of expressing his mind.

- Sextile/Trine: Unusual things interest the individual. He is smart, inventive, independent, and original.

- Square/Opposite: Erratic and rebellious, the person usually finds himself in conflict. However, his brilliant mind can solve these predicaments and take him to great lengths.

Mercury and Neptune

Mercury is for thoughts while Neptune is for imagination. These two working together can create manifested dreams and creative ideas.

- Conjunction: An all-around creative person who can be a visionary as well. The downside is that he can sometimes lose touch with reality.

- Sextile/Trine: Although highly imaginative, the person still has a discerning mind.

- Square/Opposite: He may find the need to decide between fantasy and reality. He may be highly creative but also disorganized, acknowledging only what he wants and ignoring the rest.

Mercury and Pluto

Investigative Pluto linked with smart Mercury creates a focused mind, which penetrates mysteries.

- Conjunction: Good with analysis and probing secrets, this is something that is noticeable in detectives and researchers. This can also create obsessive notions, as Pluto is a planet of obsession.

- Sextile/Trine: A creative and insightful person who has the ability to dig deeper into issues. He is flexible enough in most matters.

- Square/Opposite: Although highly intelligent, this person can be combative and obsessive.

Venus

Venus is the planet of beautiful things: art, love, relationships, possessions, and pleasure.

Venus and Mars

Venus is love and mars is passion. These two trigger invigorating encounters.

- Conjunction: A highly attractive and demonstrative person. However, he may create conflicts in relationships just to incite excitement.

- Sextile/Trine: A charismatic and loving individual who can attain fulfillment in relationships.

- Square/Opposite: The subject may be uncertain of what he truly desires, thus romantic relationships are stressful.

Venus and Jupiter

When Jupiter's generosity encounters Venus' affection, an abundance of love and pleasure ensues.

- Conjunction: Since Jupiter is a planet of luck, this is fortunate because the subject attracts good things into his way. This also bestows artistic prowess.

- Sextile/Trine: This enhances attractiveness and the ability to earn income.

- Square/Opposite: There is a tendency to blow things out of proportion. The person may overindulge in something. He may also be overly emotional.

Venus and Saturn

Venus is the planet of affection while Saturn is of control. This aspect can discipline and refine love, but it can also create suffering in relationships.

- Conjunction: Romance is treated seriously and sometimes even obsessively. The person has been hurt a lot in previous relationships, making him limit himself when it comes to love. On the other hand, this aspect also hones artistic talents.

- Sextile/Trine: Responsible and gives importance to security. Loyal to his/her partner.

- Square/Opposite: The subject may be afraid to lose something valuable to him, causing him to work extra hard to prevent that possibility. This may also trigger issues in his romantic life.

Venus and Uranus

Lovely Venus and surprising Uranus combinations create exciting romances.

- Conjunction: This makes an exciting personality and an electrifying love life.

- Sextile/Trine: Is attracted to exciting and unusual people and is one himself. He is lucky in both love and money.

- Square/Opposition: Often finds himself in unstable relationships with the wrong kind of people, or at least those who no one will expect will be suitable for him.

Venus and Neptune

Dreamy Neptune gives an otherworldly quality to Venus' charms.

- Conjunction: A vivid imagination and a talent for aesthetics can bestow a mastery of the arts and music. On the downside, this can let desires mess up with good judgement. This is also the aspect of spiritual people.

- Sextile/Trine: Although caring and creative, the subject may be lazy and self-indulgent.

- Square/Opposite: Commonly gets infatuated with someone.

Venus and Pluto

When Pluto's obsessiveness encounters Venus' passion, drama is inevitable.

- Conjunction: This aspect creates a sexually charged and dominating person. On the positive side, this also signifies

- Sextile/Trine: Although still intense, this aspect is not as destructive as others. The subject seeks to improve himself through the relationships he invests in. He also attracts powerful people into his life.

- Square/Opposite: This hard aspect makes one prone to obsessions, but can also give an irresistible appeal.

Mars

Mars is the symbol for the will, aggression and energy.

Mars and Jupiter

Jupiter's optimism mixed with Mars' vitality creates vigor and excitement.

- Conjunction: The individual always finds the energy to do what he wants to do. He knows the right time to act.

- Sextile/Trine: This bestows an adventurous spirit, which sets big dreams and accomplishes them.

- Square/Opposite: A driven and restless person, he can benefit from keeping things in moderation.

Mars and Saturn

Impulsive Mars meeting Restrained Saturn is not a harmonious pairing but they can be good for each other.

- Conjunction: This can lead the person to become inhibited, angry and self-destructive. However, it can also create discipline, persistence, and courage in the face of obstacles.

- Sextile/Trine: This inspires ambition while keeping one's feet on the ground. He can consistently achieve his goals because of his ability to make wise decisions and persevere.

- Square/Opposite: Intolerance and frustration challenge him. He may also have problems with authorities and enemies.

Mars and Uranus

Volatile Mars and quirky Uranus often cause trouble.

- Conjunction: Uninhibited and resolute, but may be prone to accidents.

- Sextile/Trine: The subject seeks extraordinary goals and new experiences. He also reacts rapidly. The negative side of this aspect is that there's a chance that one's energy may be scattered. However, since this is a harmonious aspect, he can avoid this easily.

- Square/Opposite: A rebel who tends to upset everything around him. This can create an adventurous or a destructive character.

Mars and Neptune

Driven Mars can energize Neptune's fantasies. On the other hand, Neptune's unclear perceptions can be worsened by Mars' rashness.

- Conjunction: This can lead to an unstable yet multi-talented personality. He may have a hard time directing his energy and go for goals that are impossible to achieve.

- Sextile/Trine: The subject can translate aspirations into actions by directing his talents.

- Square/Opposite: With high ideals but can be discouraged quite easily and avoid difficulties.

Mars and Pluto

Mars and Pluto are both intense planets, thus people with this aspect have a lot of ambition and the persistence to get their desires.

- Conjunction: The subject is likely to be a go-getter with an abundant supply of personal energy.

- Sextile/Trine: Confident and energetic, he can start something new with plenty of enthusiasm and work on it continuously without getting tired. He can also end something without losing his composure.

- Square/Opposite: A highly passionate person who may have problems controlling emotions and staying away from problems. Luckily, his overwhelming drive and ability to weed out negative behaviors help him achieve power.

Jupiter

Jupiter is the planet for expansion, prosperity, wisdom and luck.

Jupiter and Saturn

- Jupiter and Saturn are polar opposites, so when they are in aspect to each other, expect issues that may lead to problems, thereby helping the person become more determined.

- Conjunction: Frustration is likely when Saturn the disciplinarian dominates jovial Jupiter. The individual encounters plenty of obstacles, which will train him to work harder than most of his peers.

- Sextile/Trine: Pragmatic and reasonable, the subject knows his strong and weak points and works well with both of them. He can turn his dreams into reality.

- Square/Opposite: The individual feels torn between two extremes, resulting to discontentment and restlessness. He may distrust his own judgements.

Jupiter and Uranus

The surprise-loving Uranus boosts Jupiter's ability to give positive things to the person, thus creating unexpected luck and opportunities.

- Conjunction: An idealistic risk-taker who always experiences strokes of luck.

- Sextile/Trine: Original and creative, the subject is quick to grab opportunities in unique ways.

- Square/Opposite: There is a disdain for planning and traditional methods and prefers to make decisions by impulse. He may rebel against anything that he perceives as restrictive.

Jupiter and Neptune

The larger-than-life energy of Jupiter influences starry-eyed Neptune and creates lavish dreams, vivid imagination and deep spirituality.

- Conjunction: This is a beneficial aspect to idealism and spirituality, but this can also cause lack of focus and confusion. On the positive side, his luck makes up for his misses.

- Sextile/Trine: Kind-hearted, perceptive and creative with a penchant for spirituality.

- Square/Opposite: Since both Jupiter and Neptune are not really strong in discipline, the subject may be prone to scattering his efforts and not think hard before doing something. This can also cause escapist behavior. On the bright side, this can mean musical talent or a knack for making money.

Jupiter and Pluto

Jupiter expands things and pulls in opportunities, while Pluto transforms and penetrates.

- Conjunction: The individual has strong beliefs and wants to change the world – and can.

- Sextile/Trine: He is ready for change and can find some benefit from it. This aspect can also create an inspiring leader.

- Square/Opposition: This gives an ability to go head-to-head against formidable enemies and be victorious, thus he can also make significant changes in the world. However, he can have a lust for power and be destructive to himself and others.

Saturn

Saturn represents limitations, restrictions and discipline. This shows challenges and the things that needs to be done.

Saturn and Uranus

When limited and conforming Saturn collides with liberating and rebellious Uranus, things tend to go haywire.

- Conjunction: Because the genius of Uranus blends with the practicality of Saturn, he can channel his brilliance to actual actions. This allows him to be a wise leader.

- Sextile/Trine: The person accomplishes what he sets out for.

- Square/Opposite: Feeling a tension between two opposite forces, the subject can resort to narcissism, apathy and hypocrisy. He may feel neglected as well. However, this aspect can also turn a person into a reformer of all things outdated.

Saturn and Neptune

When grounded Saturn meets fantasy-prone Neptune, they may either heighten sensitivity or reduce clarity – according to the aspect.

- Conjunction: Disciplined and creative at the same time.

- Sextile/Trine: This makes the individual focus his imagination in practical ways.

- Square/Opposite: The person tends to be reclusive and have distrust of others. He may also be disorganized in some way – this area can be deciphered by considering the placement of Saturn.

Saturn and Pluto

Pluto is about deep change while Saturn is about hard work and discipline. This strengthens the person's ability to change himself through his own efforts.

- Conjunction: Saturn stops Pluto's impulse to change, thus, he may be prone to stubbornness, obsessions and compulsions. He needs to work persistently around his issues to go beyond this tendency.

- Sextile/Trine: This gives additional strength to his will and self-discipline.

- Square/Opposite: Although obsessions and compulsions are likely, he has enough determination to overcome them.

The Outer Planets

The outermost planets of Uranus, Neptune and Pluto move so slowly that their influence is more on generations of people rather than a particular individual. However, there are times when they are personally significant:

- When these outer planets are near each other

- When a planet is conjunct with the Ascendant or Midheaven

- When they aspect the Sun, Moon or Ascendant ruler

- When they rule the Sun sign, Moon sign or Ascendant sign

Uranus and Neptune

Revolutionary Uranus and spiritual Neptune brings inspiration.

- Conjunction: This aspect creates a nervous attitude and an original approach to social change.

- Sextile/Trine: The person belongs to a generation, which is inclined to spirituality.

- Square/Opposite: The subject is emotionally sensitive and eccentric.

Uranus and Pluto

These two power-packed planets trigger major revolutions.

- Conjunction: This aspect caused revolutions and transformations, especially those that involve rebellious creativity.

- Sextile/Trine: Uranus and Pluto interacting with each other harmoniously causes disruptive transformations, but the individual can cope with it well.

- Square/Opposite: Natural reactions to changes are suppressed, thus the generation born under this aspect are prone to be more stressed than others.

Neptune and Pluto

Neptune's vision combined with Pluto's depths launch world-changing endeavors.

- Conjunction: This creates a yearning for spirituality driven by the need for understanding and using power in the right ways.

- Sextile/Trine: This creates an interest in all things mystical, such as the new age, occult and original forms of spirituality.

- Square/Opposite: There is a strong interest in either sex or the supernatural.

This chapter dealt with the planets by themselves. The following will consider how the signs influence each of them.

CHAPTER 13

The Planets in the Zodiac Signs

The Sun

The sun reveals the characteristics of the zodiac sign where it is in. This is called the sun-sign and is discussed earlier in the book.

The Moon

- Aries: The Moon in fiery Aries results to emotional spontaneity, extreme sensitivity, enthusiasm, and dynamism.

- Taurus: The Moon in earthy Taurus gives a person sensuality, a focus on pleasures, possessiveness and attachment.

- Gemini: A Gemini moon brings diverse interests and excellent communication skills.

- Cancer: The moon in Cancer resembles a nurturing and protective mother. It also leads to a rich imagination.

- Leo: When the moon is in Leo, there is pride and a desire for perfection.

- Virgo: A Virgo moon imbues modesty and discretion and a desire to be useful, helpful and skilled.

- Libra: A moon in Libra gives sophistication and an increased taste for aesthetics.

- Scorpio: The moon in Scorpio leads to passion and intensity, whether in emotional or idealistic endeavors.

- Sagittarius: Free-spirited Sagittarius' moon gives adventure and a deep love for discovery and exploration.

- Capricorn: The moon in Capricorn provides discipline, austerity, and sound values.

- Aquarius: The Aquarius moon provokes idealism and open-mindedness to new things.

- Pisces: When the moon is in Pisces, there is a fascination with mysticism, communion and dreams. The individual may also be hypersensitive.

- The phases of the moon also have significance in a person's birth chart.

- The New Moon relates to a period of conception, creation and secrecy.

- The Waxing Moon is a gradual release of energy and symbolizes developing actions.

- The Full Moon is the peak of a progress or the moment of success or failure in an endeavor.

- The Waning Moon is an evaluative period where the person reviews what has been done or what has transpired. This also relates to reflecting on life lessons and consulting previous experiences.

The phase of the moon during birth will have lasting effects on the subject's personality. Also, the moon phase is useful in determining the best things to do and avoid during specific times.

Personal Planets

The personal planets are the closest and correspond to a person's thoughts, feelings and actions.

Mercury (thoughts and communication)

- Aries: Having a moon in Mercury results to a quick, innovative and intuitive mind, which focuses on discovering new things. It may also bestow a provocative intellect.

- Taurus: Taurus has a slow but stable energy. Mercury in this sign leads to the gradual assimilation of knowledge. There may also be a fascination towards sensual thoughts.

- Gemini: Mercury is at home in Gemini and magnifies its good qualities. It creates a great communicator and a rational analyst.

- Cancer: The sign of Cancer is more emotional than objective. Thus, when Mercury is in here, it gives a poetic mind, which is sometimes irrational.

- Leo: Perfectionist Leo imbues a belief in truth and synthesis.

- Virgo: Virgo is likewise a perfectionist, so when Mercury is in here, there is a desire to master a subject. The focus is more on analysis and technical matters, though.

- Libra: Lawyers with a genuine love for justice usually have Mercury in Libra. Their keen intelligence enables them to handle subtleties.

- Scorpio: Scorpio is all about mystery and controversy. Mercury in Scorpio can give a talent for polemics or an interest in mysteries and the occult.

- Sagittarius: Sagittarius' expansive view makes a person seek to link knowledge from different domains.

- Capricorn: Mercury in Capricorn instills a discipline in searching for meaning using relevant methods of a field.

- Aquarius: An Aquarius Mercury bestows an intuitive approach that is often based on universal principles and open-minded communication.

- Pisces: Mercury guided by Pisces gains understanding through identification with the subject.

Venus (feelings and love)

- Aries: When Venus is in Aries, the character is seductive, passionate, enthusiastic, and sometimes have an overwhelming effect on others.

- Taurus: Venus is the ruler of Taurus. This energy results into tenderness, loyalty, and attachment.

- Gemini: Gemini causes a person to have a need for intellectual exchanges when in love. It also causes one to be experimental in demonstrating affections.

- Cancer: When the love planet is in a nurturing sign, he becomes loving. It also causes one to display motherly instincts.

- Leo: Venus in Leo activates an idealistic view on love. The person regards affection as something noble and exclusive to a partner.

- Virgo: Being in Virgo, Venus brings a character that is shy and modest but compassionate and sincere. His feelings are usually guarded.

- Libra: Venus being in charming Libra results to a magnetic personality who takes pleasure in exchanges.

- Scorpio: Intense Scorpio makes a person become passionate and feel things extremely.

- Sagittarius: Expansive Sagittarius evokes overwhelming love that may surge up at times. The individual may need large spaces to handle feelings.

- Capricorn: Methodical Capricorn affects Venus so that feelings develop gradually and sequentially.

- Aquarius: Venus in Aquarius crates non-conformity and provocative love. Tender affection towards friends is commonplace.

- Pisces: Pisces love borders on the sacred.

Mars (action and aggression)

- Aries: Impulsive Aries combined with Mars causes rapid decisions and quick actions.

- Taurus: Taurus Mars is slow to take action but becomes unstoppable when momentum is gained. Anger is likewise gradual and may unfortunately lead to rage when uncontrolled.

- Gemini: Mars in Gemini makes the person disperse his anger and demonstrate little aggression. Frustration may be eloquently expressed in words but not through physical violence.

- Cancer: Mars is associated with anger; if it's in motherly Cancer, it becomes more of a pacifist. Anger is often expressed as moodiness and not outright aggression.

- Leo: Mars in Leo gifts the courage and righteousness of a hero.

- Virgo: Virgo influences Mars to be industrious and meticulous, accomplishing tasks with great care.

- Libra: Mars in peace-loving Libra dislikes arguments.

- Scorpio: Scorpio and Mars are both intense, so when they're combined, there is uncontrollable passion, making it hard for him to get exhausted.

- Sagittarius: Sagittarius' wide horizons mean that Mars obtains a desire to expend its energy without limitations.

- Capricorn: Capricorn's love for achievement makes Mars strive for mastery in attaining objectives.

- Aquarius: Mars in Aquarius creates a focus on creativity and convictions. Actions are imaginative and dedicated to worthwhile causes.

- Pisces: Mars in gentle Pisces is kind even in anger, but it can lead to passive-aggressiveness.

Social Planets

The social planets influence the social behavior of the person.

Jupiter (friendships and expansion)

- Aries: Social Jupiter in Aries leads to dynamic interactions. The individual is gifted with optimism, confidence and an involvement in life.

- Taurus: Taurus is about pleasure and prosperity. When Jupiter is in this sign, there is a sensual love for life and a drive to prosper.

- Gemini: When a person has Jupiter in child-like Gemini, he acts youthful no matter what the age.

- Cancer: The social life of those with Jupiter in Cancer is filled with kindness, charm and hospitality.

- Leo: Jupiter in Leo generates a taste for honor and success, which can be excessive at times.

- Virgo: Natural organizers and managers often have Jupiter in Virgo. They are keen to neglect nothing when completing tasks.

- Libra: Jupiter in sociable Libra can lead a person into dedicating his life into public affairs.

- Scorpio: Determined and insightful Scorpio influences Jupiter to have a knack for business.

- Sagittarius: Jupiter is Sagittarius' planet. This combination creates explorers and people who do important deeds.

- Capricorn: Jupiter in Capricorn has ambition dedicated to research and social, political or religious issues.

- Aquarius: Jupiter being in Aquarius shows a belief in democracy and the spirit of brotherhood.

- Pisces: When Jupiter is found in Pisces, the person yearns for communion with all forms of creation. He also seeks compassionate.

Saturn (conflicts and restrictions)

- Aries: When Saturn is in Aries, a person fights to achieve his goals. Stress may be heightened during this time.

- Taurus: Saturn in stubborn Taurus results to a refusal to change one's ways and opinions.

- Gemini: A Gemini Saturn addresses conflicts with objective discourse. This is also an indicator of intellectualism and rationality.

- Cancer: With Saturn in Cancer, there is a focus on the past.

There may have been some issues with the family.

- Leo: Leo in Saturn points out to a tendency to be superior to others.

- Virgo: Saturn in calculating Virgo encourages meticulous study to understand situations better.

- Libra: A Libra Saturn seeks justice and restoration of balance.

- Scorpio: Persistent Saturn in direct Scorpio results to uncompromising authenticity.

- Sagittarius: Philosophical Sagittarius causes Saturn to broaden up its views, leading to a discerning yet open-minded take on the situation.

- Capricorn: Saturn is the planet of Capricorn. This configuration is often observed in political leaders, researchers, and wise men of all kinds.

- Aquarius: Saturn's persistence joined with Aquarius' ideals creates perfectionism and a drive towards greater wisdom for all.

- Pisces: Saturn, a planet of endings, in the last Zodiac speaks of evaluations at the end of a period.

The Transpersonal Planets

They represent the way the individual accesses other realms – such as spiritual or technological.

Uranus (revolutions and breakthroughs)

- Aries: Uranus in Aries is the creative impulse and anything revolutionary.

- Taurus: Uranus is all about new things. In Taurus, it involves stabilizing something in order to create.

- Gemini: Gemini is a communicative sign. Uranus in this sign means communication and discoveries.

- Cancer: Cancer is emotional and protective. Since Uranus is about revolutions, it signifies the end of structures and traditions. It also deals with unconventional emotional expression.

- Leo: When Uranus is located in Leo, it speaks of an urgent need to create.

- Virgo: Uranus being in Virgo represents practical, daily life that leads to insights.

- Libra: Uranus in justice-loving Libra gives an overwhelming need to deal with injustice.

- Scorpio: Scorpio's destruction coupled with Uranus' disruptive nature can trigger the obliteration of obstacles in order for evolution to commence

- Sagittarius: Sagittarius' dreams are achieved by idealistic Uranus.

- Capricorn: Capricorn's influence is concentrative. When applied unto the energy of Uranus, it becomes a concentrated effort, leading to change.

- Aquarius: Aquarian energy is enlightening. Uranus in this sign portends to transformative awakenings.

- Pisces: Pisces lie in the boundaries. When Uranus is positioned here, the parson comes into contact with other realms.

Neptune (imagination and sensitivity)

- Aries: Neptune in active Aries results to inspired and idealistic actions.

- Taurus: A Taurus Neptune induces a loving nature and sensitivity to arts.

- Gemini: Rational Gemini paired with mystic Neptune makes a person who will try to rationalize irrational things.

- Cancer: Neptune within Cancer stirs a longing for emotional union.

- Leo: When Neptune is in Leo, there is divine love in one's soul.

- Virgo: Virgo Neptune applies ideals to daily living.

- Libra: Neptune in Libra describes peace and harmony.

- Scorpio: Neptune in Scorpio hints to aspirations for deep experiences

- Sagittarius: Neptune in Sagittarius announces the appearance of long lasting forms of spirituality.

- Capricorn: Neptune in no-nonsense Capricorn is being responsible for ideals.

- Aquarius: Mystical Neptune in intuitive Aquarius gives a person psychic abilities.

- Pisces: Neptune in Pisces, its home sign, signifies unity.

Pluto (transformations)

- Aries: The configuration of Pluto in Aries can lead to a person becoming a warrior or militant.

- Taurus: Pluto in Taurus embodies instinct and energy.

- Gemini: Rebellious Pluto in outspoken Gemini enables one to express what is usually left unsaid and go past taboos.

- Cancer: When in Cancer, Pluto's abundant energy is dedicated for caring endeavors.

- Leo: Powerful Pluto in prideful Leo can mean fighting against authority and establishing one's own power.

- Virgo: Virgo is associated with the physical body. Pluto in Virgo may have something to do with internal energies, particularly the Kundalini.

- Libra: Pluto is linked to domination. When it's in Libra, the sign for relationships, it can mean choosing between dominance and partnerships.

- Scorpio: Pluto is the planet of Scorpio. This formation can lead to the awakening of the Kundalini.

- Sagittarius: Since Pluto is a planet for energy, the Sagittarius influence can mean that one's energy increases.

- Capricorn: Pluto residing in Capricorn gives a strong and transformative will.

- Aquarius: When dominating Pluto finds itself in humanitarian Aquarius, an internal conflict may arise, forcing the individual to choose between dominance and selflessness.

- Pisces: When Pluto, planet of transformation, goes into Pisces, it may mean that changes may occur. It may also enhance one's psychic vibrations.

CHAPTER 14

The Ascendant

The Ascendant is the sign, which is rising on the Eastern horizon during the moment of a person's birth. This is different from the Sun sign (the one most commonly referred to in general horoscopes).

The Ascendant describes the image projected to others. It does not represent one's true personality, but how one is likely to be perceived.

Aries: Having Aries as the rising sign means having an image of being active. The person may be constantly on the move, starting several projects and invigorating people around him. This energy can sometimes be rash and impulsive, resulting to conflicts or accidents.

Taurus: A person with a Taurus ascendant gives the impression of stability. He is also viewed as reliable, generous and pleasant. Patience is one of his most positive traits. He is persistent and slow to anger. However, along with this comes stubbornness and resistance to change.

Gemini: Gemini rising influences an individual to be communicative whether in speaking, writing, or other forms of expression. He is quite intelligent, with the ability to absorb information and adapt to changing circumstances quickly. There is curiosity and a love for discovering new things, but this may mean that the person gets bored rapidly.

Cancer: A Cancer ascendant increases a person's imagination and sensitivity. This makes him become more attuned to emotions from himself and those of others, thus, he can be more perceptive than most people. Because of the nurturing attitude however, he may be taken advantage of by others. Likewise, he may not be good in decisions because he often gives way to emotions rather than reason.

Leo: Leo rising gives a magnetic influence, which is impossible to ignore. The individual loves having fun while entertaining others. He is a natural leader whom everyone wants to follow. Unlike other signs, those with a Leo ascendant lead because there is a genuine desire to help. Even though this person may have excessive pride at times, this confidence is charming enough that most people tolerate it.

Virgo: Having Virgo as the ascending sign results to an individual having a prim and proper demeanor. This behavior is a result of thoughtfulness and a perfectionistic attitude. This also allows him to handle details well and assimilate knowledge thoroughly. With a tendency to be more intellectual, he may not be good in dealing with emotional displays and prefers to hide his true feelings.

Libra: When one's ascendant sign is Libra, he is charming, polite and attractive. He may have a strong need for harmony, thus he may become aloof when there is conflict, but at the same time, seek ways to restore justice. He has a liking for arts and beautiful things. He also gives a lot of importance to partnerships of all kinds.

Scorpio: A Scorpio ascendant gives a seductive and mysterious appeal. There may be an air of secrecy around the person, but ironically, is good in probing secrets. He is an excellent persuader as well and may be ruthless when he wants to. He can transform himself and those around him.

Sagittarius: Those with Sagittarius ascending are lovers of travel and philosophy. They are generally good natured and popular with various kinds of people. Their optimism makes them take more opportunities that others normally avoid. However, they may dislike being restrained in any way, and would not hesitate to disengage when their freedom is threatened.

Capricorn: Capricorn rising gives an air of seriousness. Emotional expression is controlled and only done when needed. Ambitious and methodical, this person may become an effective leader. There is a tendency to be stressed though, as people with this ascendant may work harder than most.

Aquarius: Aquarius in the ascendant gives popularity and an interest in diverse things. The individual is pleasant but keeps his distance from people. This may seem as if he is disinterested in them, but this is because he is more intellectual rather than empathic. He also values his own freedom and will be unwilling to limit himself for the sake of others.

Pisces: Pisces rising means being sensitive to the point of being psychic. The person may feel emotions of other people so he may be unable to tolerate negative situations. Because of his connection to emotions and harmony, he may love art and have artistic skill. The inward focus presents a danger of confusing fantasy with reality. However, if this is managed, the person may have the ability to turn all his dreams into reality.

CHAPTER 15

The Descendant

The descendant is the sign, which is directly opposite of the ascendant. This gives insights into the person's relationships.

Aries (Libra ascendant): The ideal mate is a passionate person who can energize him and help come into terms with disagreements.

Taurus (Scorpio ascendant): The partner sought for is trustworthy and stable enough to withstand the outbursts of Scorpio rising.

Gemini (Sagittarius ascendant): This may mean avoiding being in a serious relationships. If ready for it, the mate is an eloquent and complex person who is fun enough to keep him hooked.

Cancer (Capricorn ascendant): A sweet and caring mate is desired by hardworking people with Capricorn rising. Relationships will tend to be conventional.

Leo (Aquarius ascendant): Someone with a fiery and entertaining personality will keep the interest of emotionally detached people with Aquarius rising.

Virgo (Pisces ascendant): A practical and analytical partner is a good match to a dreamy and sometimes careless person with Pisces rising.

Libra (Aries ascendant): Equality is valued in relationships. The ideal partner is someone who is even-keeled to counteract impulsiveness.

Scorpio (Taurus ascendant): There is a craving for a partner who is intense, sexual and intimate. This may also attract partners who are dominating, manipulative, and secretive.

Sagittarius (Gemini ascendant): He seeks a partner who is free-spirited and can expand his views. He may marry more than once.

Capricorn (Cancer ascendant): Practicality and reliability are top priorities in a mate. A healthy relationship provides a feeling of security.

Aquarius (Leo ascendant): The perfect partner for the adventurous folks with Leo rising is someone who is unique and intellectually stimulating.

Pisces (Virgo ascendant): A sensitive and calming person will be excellent for the anxious perfectionists with Virgo rising.

CHAPTER 16

The Midheaven

The Midheaven is the highest point in the birth chart. This has effects on the person's public persona, status, career trends and attitude towards authority and powerful people. This also tells something about one of the person's biological parents.

Aries: The individual approaches things with courage, thus he tends to start many projects and take more risks. However, he does not want to be told what to do, so careers where he is his own boss will be more suitable.

Taurus: Having Taurus in MC provides the fortitude that will eventually yield rewards in the career. There is a preference for doing something concrete and practical.

Gemini: Intellectually stimulating careers are favored, and there may be a fair amount of writing or expression involved. Taking trips may be needed for a job to be satisfying.

Cancer: Ideal work makes use of intuition and emotional sensitivity. They may strive to provide security not only for themselves, but also for those whom they work with.

Leo: The work may bring public recognition and avenues for creative expression. There may be leadership positions offered. The most satisfying jobs are those where their efforts are appreciated.

Virgo: Success at work is brought about by meticulous hard work. There is a danger of doing too much, even when he is not recognized or compensated.

Libra: Careers involving rational and harmonious work are ideal. Social interactions are frequent. Working may include exposure to the arts and other aesthetic matters. The individual may attract helpful people.

Scorpio: Work, which is intense in some way, are appealing. He may find himself in positions of authority or that involves exerting control over others. There is determination in working that will enable success.

Sagittarius: The person is drawn to professions that carry opportunities to expand horizons. He may be recognized for his convictions. Although authorities are usually helpful to the individual, he may not appreciate being controlled.

Capricorn: Commitment is given to the work regardless of how difficult it is. Because of the craving for structure, the individual may thrive in a corporate environment. There is a tendency for depression though, so it is advisable for him to appreciate the good things in his job.

Aquarius: The individual seeks work that helps the larger community. He may be involved in unconventional tasks that are suitable to his unique characteristics. Progress is prioritized.

Pisces: Career duties often make use of imagination and creativity. They may also entail helping and caring for others. Aesthetic expression may also be part of the job, thus, singers, artists and dancers may have Pisces in MC. Because Pisces deals with the mysterious, the individual may also be drawn toward psychic or occult work.

CHAPTER 17

The Nadir

The IC is opposite the MC and it portrays the person's approach to his family and home.

Aries: The person energizes himself when he is at home. He may also get into frequent fights with other members of the family.

Taurus: Financial security, and stability are prioritized in the family. The home is designed for maximum pleasure and comfort.

Gemini: The home is usually filled with communication gadgets and informational materials (books, encyclopedias, etc.) The person may have two homes.

Cancer: There are strong ties to the family, especially the mother. He may have a strong desire to live near bodies of water.

Leo: The home is a place where the person can let his inner light shine. He is proud of his house and family.

Virgo: The home area is clean and organized, but he may move a lot until he finds the perfect place to live in. Domestic life is a stabilizing influence to the person.

Libra: A harmonious family life takes top priority. The home tends to be beautiful and peaceful.

Scorpio: The home is considered as a safe place where intense emotions are expressed and deep needs are met.

Sagittarius: The family may have a set of beliefs that have shaped the person considerably. There may be frequent changes of residences, or there may be a longing to move far away. The home may be perceived as a place to feel free.

Capricorn: The person may carry a heavy responsibility for the family, which is likely to be conservative. The home is traditionally styled and designed for security.

Aquarius: The home or the things in it may be unusual. Family life is non-traditional, or at least his approach towards it.

Pisces: The house may be a spiritual haven. He may be abandoned during childhood, thus, the present home is geared towards providing a sense of union with the others in it.

The final chapter of this book will discuss how astrology predictions figure into our future.

CHAPTER 18

Knowing What the Future Holds with Astrology Predictions

One of the common uses of astrology is to predict the future. This is done by interpreting planetary movements in relation to other galactic bodies during a certain point in time. Can astrology be an accurate tool to predict the future? Many are skeptics and consider that astrology predictions are not any better than a simple coin toss. However, the number of adherents is not to be disregarded because many still cling to the prospect of knowing what the future has in store for them.

There are various techniques used by astrologers to look into the future of a person. Followers of any of these techniques, in whatever complex method they work, assert that these tools are good means to give predictions and guide them in making plans for tomorrow. Here are some of the preferred techniques in making astrology predictions to cause the future present itself before it even unfolds.

Transit and Cycles

An individual's natal chart is like being photographed from the sky the moment he is born. It stays with him throughout the course of his life as intergalactic bodies continue to move in cycles. As these movements happen, special relationships are formed between them that produce forces and effects to the person's natal chart. To determine this occurrence, astrological transits are used to predict trends and developments in the future. It is used to interpret planet movement as they continuously transit the horoscope. Transits act as stimulus in triggering a person's psychological being.

In getting an overview of the future, it is best to look initially at the outer planet transits and cycles before fine-tuning predictions with the inner planet transits and cycles. Outer planets are those slow-moving transits that have a huge impact in a person's natal chart. Having a perspective from the outside in is best because this offers an extensive impression of the transits and conditions. This provides astrology predictions better options to be used for refinements that can be generated from the inner planet transits.

The positions of the planets at the moment of birth are not the only ones exerting an effect on a subject – progressions do too. Progressions are planetary positions after a given period of time. This new arrangement forms aspects or "transits" with the planets' locations at birth and other crucial elements of the birth chart.

The things that will be considered in the transits are the following:

- Aspects to the natal planets

- Aspects to the ascendant and/or mid-heaven

- Aspects to the houses

The transits that matter the most are those made by the outermost planets, since they move slower and have longer influence. The effects are more prominent when they are transiting the inner planets.

Mars Transits

Mars is energy and aggression. Transits to Mars create a need for assertiveness and activity that can also trigger movement. However, because this is considered as a minor planet, it usually affects only minor events in life.

- First house: There is a forward drive, which is good for starting tasks, but arguments are likely as well.

- Second house: The activity is directed to money: whether earning or spending.

- Third house: Energy is available for communication matters and short trips. There's a possibility of quarrelling.

- Fourth house: Working around the house is recommended, but tensions with others also living in the house may happen.

- Fifth house: A good time for activities involving leisure, children and romance, but the person needs to watch out for sports-induced injuries.

- Sixth house: This transit encourages work of all kinds. Avoid conflicts at work.

- Seventh house: Mars can remove conflicts in relationships but at the same time, create new ones. It can also instigate connections.

- Eight house: Mars may enhance sexual desire. Be careful of being impulsive in borrowing money or having sexual relations.

- Ninth House: This is ideal for going on long trips. However, it can provoke debates on ideas.

- Tenth House: A fortunate time for doing something related to work, business and career. Just avoid problems with parents, authorities, or superiors.

- Eleventh House: There is energy for making new friends and connections, as well as fulfilling wishes. Watch out for disputes with peers.

- Twelfth House: Take caution because the 12th house is about limitations and problems, and Mars may activate those. Don't do anything significant this time.

- Natal Sun: Good for beginning things, but hard aspects can lead to a feeling of being overwhelmed. Arguments with men are possible.

- Natal Moon: Emotions may be active. Arguments with women are likely.

- Natal Mercury: Communication tasks are much easier but can also cause argumentativeness.

- Natal Venus: This can lead to romance or a passion for arts.

- Natal Mars: Provides extra energy for physical pursuits. Be careful of illnesses and accidents.

- Natal Jupiter: This can lead to over-enthusiasm and carelessness.

- Natal Saturn: This combination is ideal for focusing on a task or planning for a battle. However, be careful of run-ins with superiors and accidents with sharp items.

- Natal Uranus: This can trigger abrupt changes whether for good or for bad. Take care not to rush things to avoid mishaps.

- Natal Neptune: Good for artistic and charitable activities. However, this can lead to deceptions and delusions.

- Natal Pluto: This may attract violence to the individual, but it's also an excellent period to do something challenging or let go of unhelpful things.

- Natal Ascendant: Harmonious aspects are good for launching new projects, but hard aspects are for continuing with ongoing tasks. For an opposition, others' lack of cooperation may be an issue.

- Natal Midheaven: Suitable for expending energy at home or in the career or having a productive argument with bosses.

Jupiter Transits

Because Jupiter brings good luck, transits to Jupiter are generally fortunate. However, the positivity associated with this planet may lead to overindulgence and carelessness. It may also expand something – such as your waistline.

- First house: The first house is for appearance so it can literally make you bigger – take care not to overeat. Since Jupiter is the ruler of Sagittarius, it may also give you an edge on intellectual and philosophical matters.

- Second house: Expect boosts on your wealth but take care not to overspend.

- Third house: Relationships may improve, especially with people close to you literally and symbolically. Communications may flow more smoothly. Learning concrete subjects is easier.

- Fourth house: This aspect is good for matters dealing with the home.

- Fifth house: Expect good things with recreations, children and romance.

- Sixth house: Fortunate events related to work may arrive.

- Seventh house: This transit is good for relationships, including business deals.

- Eight house: Jupiter in the eight house may make borrowing money easier and sex more enjoyable.

- Ninth House: Abstract subjects will be more understandable at this time. Long travels will be comfortable and fulfilling. It is also a good chance to publish something.

- Tenth House: A fortunate moment to advance in the career. This can also add to publicity or improve one's reputation.

- Eleventh House: The circle of friends will grow bigger. Helpful people will enter the subject's life.

- Twelfth House: The twelfth house is for enemies and harmful things. Jupiter in this house may protect the subject from these things.

- Natal Sun: This is a fortunate transit even among the hard aspects. It's recommended to expand horizons – literally or symbolically.

- Natal Moon: Jupiter in the planet of emotions can make one feel good. This is also good for domestic affairs.

- Natal Mercury: Hard aspects (square and opposite) may lead to loss of focus and impulsive talking.

- Natal Venus: Jupiter and Venus are both helpful planets, thus, they may make things easier overall.

- Natal Mars: Energy and enthusiasm is increased so the subject can get things accomplished. Stressful aspects may lead to heated discussions though.

- Natal Jupiter: Jupiter transiting the natal Jupiter can lead to overconfidence and extremely good feelings, leading to mistakes.

- Natal Saturn: This can strengthen depression, although it can also support one's self-control.

- Natal Uranus: The desire for new experiences and independence becomes stronger. There may also be some kind of unexpected fortune.

- Natal Neptune: Creativity and fantasies are likely to increase.

- Natal Pluto: This tends to exaggerate fanaticism, but it is also conducive for studying deep subjects.

- Natal Ascendant: Jupiter transits to the Ascendant may cause one to gain weight. They can also enhance sociability and trust of other people.

- Natal Midheaven: This can provoke a string of fortunate events with career, public image or the home. This can also entice interest in a cause.

Saturn Transits

- Saturn is the planet for order and effort. It's also about hard lessons and reaping what is sown.

- First house: This can last around 14 years. The transit forces the subject to focus on one's self and form his own personal identity and sense of purpose.

- Second house: Saturn in the house of value can mean having less than what's needed or not being satisfied with what one has.

- Third house: This may lead to problems with siblings and people living near you. Depression and communication issues may also arise.

- Fourth house: Changes of direction may be imminent. Problems with one parent may occur or resurface.

- Fifth house: Challenges related to creativity and sports may ensue. Romantic relationships may take on a serious flavor.

- Sixth house: This can lead to illnesses so it's an ideal time to go to check-ups. Also, defining moments in work and business may take place.

- Seventh house: Relationships may be tested at this time. The subject will start to receive the results of his own hard work.

- Eight house: The subject may encounter difficulties with credit, inheritance, or others' possessions and money. There may be sexual dysfunctions or a need for greater control in sex.

- Ninth House: Long travels are not advised in general, but this transit may be good for business trips and other serious purposes. The subject may also be forced to study something.

- Tenth House: Problems with career or authorities may occur or reappear if they were swept under the rug. This will leave the subject with no choice but to do his best in his career. However, he should not neglect other areas of life.

- Eleventh House: The subject will know who his true friends are. He may also get more responsibilities in his organization/s.

- Twelfth House: This transit is perfect for ending things. It can also bring in people who will ask for help but harm you in some way.

- Natal Sun: Conjunctions are ideal for starting things that the subject intends to stick with him for a long time. He may also experience the results of his past efforts.

- Natal Moon: The subject may have emotional problems. It can also signify the need to address issues about the home and/or real estate.

- Natal Mercury: This transit can trigger depressing ideas that may be counteracted by doing something productive.

- Natal Venus: Problems with relationships or money/resources may occur.

- Natal Mars: This can make the subject feel drained. Harmonious aspects may only cause him to focus his strength where needed.

- Natal Jupiter: This cancels out Jupiter's luck, but this may also mean that the individual will be willing to work harder.

- Natal Saturn: Saturn transiting itself can impel one to break free from limitations.

- Natal Uranus: Obstacles to dreams become more evident. The individual is tasked to make careful changes to his approaches.

- Natal Neptune: Dreams and illusions become viewed more realistically.

- Natal Pluto: The subject may find himself in the midst of power struggles. This may also help him to focus his power on worthwhile causes.

- Natal Ascendant: Discipline will be the main priority of the individual. He can expect culminating events involving his personal identity or his relationships.

- Natal Midheaven: There is likely to be a turning point in one's career or home life.

Uranus Transits

Uranus gives an erratic influence. It can spark changes – creating something new or revising old ways.

- First house: This is often a great time to make positive changes.

- Second house: Income may become unstable at this point. There may be monetary gains though when the source of income is from electronics or anything modern and unique.

- Third house: The subject may be prone to shocking other people during this transit. Siblings and neighbors may become weird. This is great for learning something new.

- Fourth house: Uranus transits in the fourth house also affects the tenth house, implying abrupt changes at work or at home.

- Fifth house: Children may become rebellious during this transit. Or, the subject may find himself dating someone he does not normally prefer. He may also become extra creative.

- Sixth house: Employees may become rebellious. This may also lead to job termination. The subject may develop a sudden illness or take interest in novel methods to take care of his health.

- Seventh house: The subject may attract eccentric people who will shake his/her world. This is not good for establishing long-term relationships with them though, as they may be unreliable.

- Eight house: There is more inventiveness in sex and loans.

- Ninth House: A recommended time to study unusual and cutting-edge subjects. It can also give a desire to travel to exotic locations.

- Tenth House: The subject may change his public image or desire greater independence from authorities.

- Eleventh House: Old groups and friends may stop being interesting or behave strangely. The individual may then find interest in new people, especially unusual ones.

- Twelfth House: This can help speed up the rate at which hidden and subconscious material is brought to awareness. Also, it can aggravate problems by making the subject more impulsive.

- Natal Sun: This can help the subject shake unhelpful things loose and escape a rut. However, this can also spell accidents.

- Natal Moon: The women in the subject's life may behave in unusual ways. Emotions may go haywire. There may be an urge to change something in the home.

- Natal Mercury: The subject needs to be careful of saying something he may regret later on. He may also be launched into studying something he has not taken interest before.

- Natal Venus: Love affairs may have an unusual element to them.

- Natal Mars: Because there is a tendency for intolerance and aggression, the subject should watch out for potential mishaps.

- Natal Jupiter: This particular transit may cause errors in judgement.

- Natal Saturn: Uranus transiting the Natal Saturn may reduce the subject's sense of security.

- Natal Uranus: There may be a compelling urge to change something.

- Natal Neptune: The subject is advised to guard against taking interest in delusions. He may benefit from a surge of imaginativeness, though.

- Natal Pluto: Clearing out will receive a tremendous boost.

- Natal Ascendant: Since this also affects the descendant, this is not a good time to make lasting commitments with others. The subject will have a greater than normal need to be independent.

- Natal Midheaven: There may be a calling to change something about the career or the home.

Neptune Transits

Neptune gives a dreamy and often illusory touch to the things it affects.

- First house: This may spark a longing to take care of others. It can also result to distractedness and tendency to daydream.

- Second house: The subject needs to be extra careful with finances.

- Third house: Since Neptune benefits imagination, this is good for creative endeavors but not detail-oriented ones.

- Fourth house: There is a danger of being confused with matters pertaining to the home or the parents.

- Fifth house: Misunderstandings with children are likely. The subject may likewise fall in love with the wrong people.

- Sixth house: Confusion with employees or service personnel is likely to happen. Diseases may be difficult to diagnose.

- Seventh house: The subject must avoid being deceived by other people or having false notions about them.

- Eight house: Partnership and credit matters may become unclear or deceptive. Sexual fantasies may become magnified.

- Ninth House: This is beneficial for creative, abstract, and spiritual pursuits.

- Tenth House: Work involving compassion, imagination, and vision may be expected during this transit.

- Eleventh House: Dreamy, eccentric individuals may enter the subject's life. He should avoid having dreams that he may never be able to attain. He should likewise refrain from helping others and neglecting his own welfare.

- Twelfth House: Because Neptune rules the twelfth house, the subject may actually eliminate his illusions. He also benefits from inspired imagination and compassion.

- Natal Sun: The subject is cautioned against delusion, substance abuse, and faulty notions.

- Natal Moon: This can increase the strength of one's own emotions and the sensitivity to others'. The subject may be more receptive to women. He/she may also become more psychic.

- Natal Mercury: The subject's thoughts become extra imaginative. He may become more persuasive to others or be more easily persuaded.

- Natal Venus: There is a tendency to view things to be better than they actually are.

- Natal Mars: The person may be compelled to act on his dreams, but this can also mean putting more effort in wishful thinking than real-world action.

- Natal Jupiter: This gives a person the tendency to focus more on dreams and the bigger picture rather than the details.

- Natal Saturn: This can obliterate the feeling of security, but one way to work around this is to ground one's dreams into reality.

- Natal Uranus: Old views will be revamped. Unusual subjects will become more interesting to the subject.

- Natal Neptune: The subject's imagination and kind-heartedness will get an immense boost.

- Natal Pluto: There is a possibility of being obsessed with dreams and delusions.

- Natal Ascendant: The subject is advised to be extra careful in not falling to delusion about one's self and other people. On the plus side, intuition may become strengthened.

- Natal Midheaven: This transit may support the career by enhancing imagination and sensitivity.

Pluto Transits

Pluto has an intense effect on the things it touches. It involves death and rebirth, and clearing out to make way for the new.

- First house: This can make the subject become more assertive or be dominated by others. This can also make him more perceptive of things.

- Second house: The subject may find himself earning money through devious means. He may also change his views about the things he values.

- Third house: Fights with siblings and other people close by are likely. Transformations with intimate relationships are expected at this time. The subject may be more persuasive when expressing himself.

- Fourth house: Since Pluto is a planet of destruction, the subject needs to insure things in his home. He should also guard himself against career troubles.

- Fifth house: Relationships may be plagued with obsession, jealousy and intrigues. There is a risk of domineering children. Caution with leisure activities is recommended.

- Sixth house: Pluto may bring health problems or obsessions with health. There may be politics with subordinates or co-workers, and other issues that may lead to job loss.

- Seventh house: Relationships are more prone to power struggles and dishonest activities.

- Eight house: This amplifies his fortune with sex and credit.

- Ninth House: There may be an intense passion and obsession with ideals. Long trips to mysterious places are anticipated. The subject may begin to study mysterious topics.

- Tenth House: The subject may experience extreme events in his career.

- Eleventh House: Friendships may either transform or be released. The subject may develop intense focus that may develop into obsessions.

- Twelfth House: Buried issues will make their way up to the surface. Hidden enemies may make themselves known.

- Natal Sun: This transit may either overwhelm the subject or energize him. This is good for transformations and releasing unwanted behaviors.

- Natal Moon: This can release repressed emotions and increase perceptiveness on emotional issues.

- Natal Mercury: The subject can investigate secrets better. His words may take power. This could also mean being more vulnerable to others' words, though.

- Natal Venus: Lovers and partners may become manipulative or aggressive. Sex drive may intensify. Hidden desires may likewise strengthen and create problems.

- Natal Mars: This aspect can drag out suppressed hostility. It can lead to explosive bursts of energy as well.

- Natal Jupiter: Belief systems may be dismantled and rebuilt. If not, the subject may become a fanatic of one.

- Natal Saturn: Pluto can activate fear or discipline. Fortunately, the individual can choose which. He can also take on a long-term commitment for beneficial change.

- Natal Uranus: This provokes the greatest changes in the subject's life.

- Natal Neptune: Delusions may die during this transit. Perceptiveness increases immensely.

- Natal Pluto: The subject's sex life may drastically improve. Other than that, he may experience being obsessed or vehement about something.

- Natal Ascendant: This transit encourages one to be more assertive, otherwise other people will force him to be so.

- Natal Midheaven: Long-lasting changes at home or in one's career are likely to happen when Pluto transits the Natal Midheaven.

Solar Returns

The Solar Return charts use charts that are calculated at the precise point when the sun returns to its original position (to happen within two days of a person's birthday). This works very much like natal charts but the effect works only within the span of a year. As the name implies, this technique largely depends on the condition of the sun and its position relative to us, our house, business address, and other areas where we want to determine the physical and external prospects. It also factors the moon's aspect in determining emotional vicissitudes focusing mainly on love and relationship. It completely guides a person on how to become rational and in control of his feelings.

Unlike the natal charts, solar return charts are transient. This means that the readings are not likely to persist after a year. For example, if a person wants to determine financial prospects, he can observe the return's second and eighth house and how the planet Venus acts. If Venus rules the house and is opposite planet Neptune, a future of instability and less materialism awaits the person. However, a better future can be expected after the charts lose their effect after a year.

Other predictive techniques exist and present themselves to be accurate in knowing a person's future. Precise or not, the important factor lies in their ability to challenge and put pressure to affect some changes in the life of an individual. They may bring good tidings but at times, may produce scary prospects. Overall, they help people to collect themselves and face whatever astrology predictions reveal what lies ahead.

Conclusion

Thank you again for purchasing this book!

I hope this book was able to help you understand the origin of astrology, the basis for horoscopes, and how both can help in important aspects of your life.

The next step is to keep an open mind and try to apply the things you learned in this book. Let these things guide you, and watch how your life would turn around.

Finally, if you enjoyed this book, please take the time to share your thoughts and post a review on Amazon. I want to reach as many people as I can with this book, and more reviews will help me accomplish that. It'd be greatly appreciated!

Thank you and good luck!

Janet Ritchie

Made in the USA
Coppell, TX
03 October 2022